These Are Friends
of Jesus

These Are
Friends
of Jesus

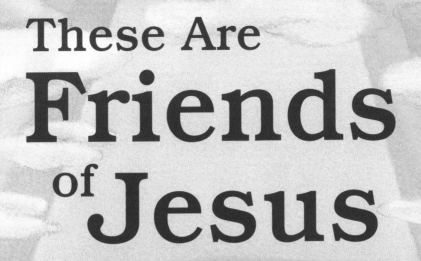

by Shirley Neitzel
Illustrated by Benrei Huang

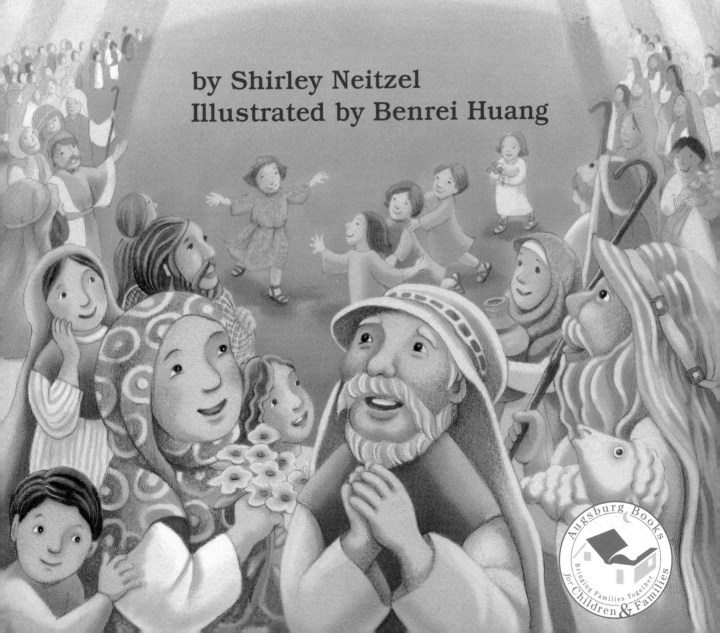

Augsburg Books

Bringing Families Together
for Children & Families

In memory of my parents,
Theophilus F. Koehler and
Ida A. Wegner Koehler —S. N.

To Amy, a cousin and a very
dear friend. —B. H.

THESE ARE FRIENDS OF JESUS

Text copyright © 2006 Shirley Neitzel. Illustrations copyright © 2006 Benrei
Huang. All rights reserved. Except for brief quotations in critical articles or
reviews, no part of this book may be reproduced in any manner without prior
written permission from the publisher. Write to: Permissions, Augsburg Fortress,
Publishers, P. O. Box 1209, Minneapolis, MN 55440-1209.

Large-quantity purchases or custom editions of this book are available at a
discount from the publisher. For more information, contact the sales department
at Augsburg Fortress, Publishers, 1-800-328-4648, or write to: Sales Director,
Augsburg Fortress, Publishers, P. O. Box 1209, Minneapolis, MN 55440-1209.

Library of Congress Cataloging-in-Publication Data
Neitzel, Shirley.
These are friends of Jesus / by Shirley Neitzel ; illustrated by Benrei Huang.
p. cm.
ISBN 0-8066-5119-9 (pbk. : alk. paper)
1. Jesus Christ—Friends and associates—Juvenile literature. I. Huang, Benrei. II.
Title.
BT302.N36 2006
232.9'5—dc22   2005010459

Cover and book design by Sarah Olmanson and Michelle L. N. Cook

The paper used in this publication meets the minimum requirements of American
National Standard for Information Sciences—Permanence of Paper for Printed
Library Materials, ANSI Z329.48-1984. ∞™

Manufactured in China.

09   08   07   06   05   1   2   3   4   5   6   7   8   9   10

God sent Jesus, his only son,
to be a friend to everyone.
Come, meet some friends of Jesus.

These are the shepherds who heard the news
that God sent Jesus, his only son,
to be a friend to everyone,
    who were joyful friends of Jesus.

These are the teachers, amazed by his views,
who, like the shepherds who heard the news
that God sent Jesus, his only son,
to be a friend to everyone,
      were thoughtful friends of Jesus.

These are disciples, the "fishers of men,"
who, like the teachers, amazed by his views,
and the shepherds who heard the news
that God sent Jesus, his only son,
to be a friend to everyone,
    were loyal friends of Jesus.

These are the sick, made well again,
who, like the disciples, the "fishers of men,"
and the teachers, amazed by his views,
and the shepherds who heard the news
that God sent Jesus, his only son,
to be a friend to everyone,
    were vigorous friends of Jesus.

These are the thousands, who all were fed,
who, like the sick, made well again,
and the disciples, the "fishers of men,"
and the teachers, amazed by his views,
and the shepherds who heard the news
that God sent Jesus, his only son,
to be a friend to everyone,
    were grateful friends of Jesus.

These are the people, raised from the dead,
who, like the thousands who were fed,
and the sick, made well again,
and the disciples, the "fishers of men,"
and the teachers, amazed by his views,
and the shepherds who heard the news
that God sent Jesus, his only son,
to be a friend to everyone,
    were spirited friends of Jesus.

These are the blind he allowed to see,
who, like the people, raised from the dead,
and the thousands who were fed,
and the sick, made well again,
and the disciples, the "fishers of men,"

and the teachers, amazed by his views,
and the shepherds who heard the news
that God sent Jesus, his only son,
to be a friend to everyone,
were thankful friends of Jesus.

These are the children, blessed at his knee,
who, like the blind he allowed to see,
and the people, raised from the dead,
and the thousands who were fed,
and the sick, made well again,
and the disciples, the "fishers of men,"
and the teachers, amazed by his views,
and the shepherds who heard the news
that God sent Jesus, his only son,
to be a friend to everyone,
      were loving friends of Jesus.

This is the thief who was forgiven,
who, like the children, blessed at his knee,
and the blind he allowed to see,
and the people, raised from the dead,
and the thousands who were fed,
and the sick, made well again,
and the disciples, the "fishers of men,"
and the teachers, amazed by his views,
and the shepherds who heard the news
that God sent Jesus, his only son,
to be a friend to everyone,
    was a humble friend of Jesus.

These are the women who heard, "He's risen!"
who, like the thief who was forgiven,
and the children, blessed at his knee,
and the blind he allowed to see,
and the people, raised from the dead,
and the thousands who were fed,

and the sick, made well again,
and the disciples, the "fishers of men,"
and the teachers, amazed by his views,
and the shepherds who heard the news
that God sent Jesus, his only son,
to be a friend to everyone,
   were faithful friends of Jesus.

These are some people who heard God's word and worshiped his Son as Savior and Lord.

They all are true friends of Jesus.

How Do We Know about Jesus' Life?

Some of Jesus' disciples wrote about things that Jesus did and said. You can find their stories in the Bible by looking up the chapters and verses listed.

God sent Jesus, his only son . . .

Isaiah 7:14; Matthew 1:18-25; Luke 1:26-35, 2:1-7; John 3:16

For hundreds of years prophets said God would send a savior to the world. The people of Israel looked forward to his coming. So when the angel Gabriel came to Mary and told her to name her baby *Jesus* she knew her son was the promised one.

These are the shepherds who heard the news . . .

Luke 2:8-20

Angels told shepherds the Savior had been born. The shepherds hurried to Bethlehem and, when they had seen the baby, told the good news to everyone they met.

These are the teachers, amazed by his views . . .

Luke 2:41-47

When he was twelve, Jesus went to Jerusalem with his parents for the feast of the Passover. On their way home, Mary and Joseph realized Jesus was not with their family or friends. They went back and found him in the temple. The teachers he was talking with were amazed by the questions he asked and his understanding of their answers.

These are disciples, the "fishers of men" . . .

Matthew 4:18-22, Mark 1:16-20, Luke 5:1-11

Jesus chose twelve men to be his disciples. The first four, Peter, Andrew, James, and John, were fishermen. Jesus told them to follow him and said, "From now on you will catch men." So they helped him tell people about God.

These are the sick, made well again . . .

Matthew 8:2-3, 9:2-7, 9:20-22; Mark 1:29-31, 40-45, 2:1-12, 5:25-34; Luke 4:38-40, 5:12-13, 18-25, 8:43-48

There are many stories of Jesus healing people. Jesus cured Simon Peter's mother-in-law's fever just by telling it to go away. Men with leprosy also were cured with just a few words. People heard these stories and came to be healed. A man who wasn't able to walk couldn't get through the crowd, so his friends took him to the roof and lowered his bed through the ceiling. Jesus cured him. A woman was healed just by touching his clothes.

These are the thousands who all were fed . . .

Matthew 14:15-21, 15:32-38; Mark 6:30-44, 8:1-10; Luke 9:10-17; John 6:1-14

Once when Jesus was talking to about five thousand people, his disciples said he should send the people away to get food. Jesus told them to give the people something to eat. They said all they had was five loaves of bread and two fish. Jesus blessed the food, and it became enough to feed everyone. Another time a crowd of four thousand was fed with seven loaves and a few fish.

These are the people, raised from the dead . . .

Matthew 9:18-26; Mark 5:21-23, 35-43; Luke 8:41-42, 49-55; John 11:1-44

Jesus saw a funeral procession at the city of Nain. He felt sorry for the man's mother, so he touched the coffin. The man sat up. He was no longer dead.

Jairus begged Jesus to come to his house because his daughter was sick. Before they got there, she had died. Jesus took her hand and spoke to her. She became alive again.

Martha and Mary sent for Jesus when their brother was sick. By the time he came to their home, Lazarus had been dead four days.

Jesus went to the tomb and called, "Come out." And Lazarus did.

These are the blind he allowed to see . . .

Matthew 9:27-31, 20:29-34; Mark 8:22-25, 10:46-52; Luke 18:35-43; John 9:1-11

With just a touch of his hand, Jesus made blind people see.

These are the children, blessed at his knee . . .

Matthew 18:2-5, 19:13-15; Mark 9:36-37, 10:13-16; Luke 18:15-17

The disciples didn't think people should bother Jesus by bringing children to him, but he wanted them to come to him. He said the love and trust of little children is like the kingdom of God.

This is the thief who was forgiven . . .

Luke 23:39-43

Jesus was crucified with two thieves. One of them admitted he deserved to be punished for his crime. He called Jesus *Lord* and asked him to remember him when he went to heaven. Jesus told him, "You will be with me."

These are the women who heard, "He's risen" . . .

Matthew 28:1-8, Mark 16:1-7, Luke 24:1-10, John 20:11-18

On the third day after Jesus was crucified, some women went to his tomb. They were surprised to find the stone that sealed it had been rolled away. An angel told them, "He is risen!" So they ran and told his disciples the news.

These are some people who heard God's word . . .

Luke 11:28

Jesus said, "Blessed are they who hear the word of God and obey it." This is as true today as it was when he said it two thousand years ago.